This Fierce Afterglow

This Fierce Afterglow

Swep Lovitt

MADVILLE
PUBLISHING

Lake Dallas, Texas

FIRST EDITION

Requests for permission to reprint or reuse material from this work should be sent to:

Permissions
Madville Publishing
PO Box 358
Lake Dallas, TX 75065

PUBLICATION CREDITS:
Many thanks to the editors of the following publications in which the poems in this collection have appeared, sometimes in previous versions. *Sometimes the World Is Too Beautiful*, Texas Review Press (2011); *A Boy's Face with Swan Wings*, UKA Press (2004), and in the following journals and anthologies: *Anemone, Asheville Poetry Review, California Quarterly, Mississippi Review, New Collage Magazine, New Jersey Poetry Journal, New South Writing, New York Quarterly, Piedmont Literary Review, Poem, Poetry Motel, Sam Houston Literary Review, Small Pond, The Texas Review, Visions-International, Brown Dog, Voices from the Web 2004, Voices from the Web 2006, Voices from the Web 2007, Voices from the Web 2008*, and *The Southern Poetry Anthology: vol. 2, Mississippi*, Texas Review Press (2010).

Cover Art: Jeremy Lovitt
Cover Design: Jeremy Lovitt

ISBN: 978-1-948692-70-0 paper, and 978-1-948692-71-7 ebook
Library of Congress Control Number: 2020946923

for my boys, Swep IV and Jeremy,
and for Jerene and Erin, always

Table of Contents

I.

II.

III.

IV.

This Fierce Afterglow

I.

PERSONAL AD UPDATE

My sexuality still won't let me
Alone, drives me to smart,
Erratic women. When I think
Of aging, I think of the Greek
Poet Seferis, calling a blood clot
A beautiful little ruby
On his brain. No longer
The post-divorce rented rooms,
A two-story white house,
Woods, beds of purple azaleas.
The Friedlaenders hung.
A blue jay on a branch just off
My porch. 2012—2019.
Seven years I've lived alone.

TO OUR SON, SWEP IV

after frictions with his mother

When you watch your eldest,
Swep V, bash baseballs,
Run around the backyard like a maniac,
Arms full, climb the big chair
To read 14 books with Pops—
Remember, *you* were *our* little boy.
As you love him, we loved you.
Your mother vomiting blood,
Refusing to go to the hospital until
Your football game had ended.

BATTING PRACTICE

Working nights, sleeping days,
When the boys filed off
The bus from school, I'd get up.
Then, bats, gloves, three
Blocks to the Kennedy Park fields,
A tall, gray painter's bucket
With forty balls, the boys
To shag for each other. Swep
Attacked each of his balls,
Sent Jeremy chasing to all corners
Of the lot. I stayed on
Jeremy, left-handed, pitch
By pitch, to pull the ball,
Discover his power.
5 p.m., the boys plopped down,
While I jogged the field
For balls missed in the clover.

JERENE ENTERED

The hospital vomiting blood.
I don't breathe until the doctor
Assures us she'll be okay.
Then, faced with a two-week stay,
And me having to work,
My parents came to pick up Swep 8,
Jeremy 5, take them back home
To Mississippi. As Mother
Packed Jeremy's bear in the trunk,
Face down, big, gray eyes up,
Jeremy said, "No, Maha,
Kirby is too little to be locked
In the dark all by himself."

MATES

I asked the boys,
A rough circle of twelve
Fifteen-year-olds,
Triangles of sweat
Soaking the backs of their shirts,
Two hours just done
In the July Tennessee sun,
I asked the boys—
And Timmy not a favorite
Of either coach, or mate—
What if a gorilla
Crashed out of the woods
Behind left field
And beelined for Timmy,
What do you boys think—
And they roared,
"That fucking gorilla
Is in trouble."

COLLABORATION

A canvas attributed to both artist
And her three-year-old, Clara.
Purple and orange across
The center in crayon. "I only left
The room for a few seconds,
Came back, and Clara's beaming."
So, *not for sale,* Clara says,
The swirls of color are unicorns—
Anything is possible—
Come out in pairs to graze at dusk.

MESSAGE IN A BOTTLE

A wicker rocker on my screen porch.
Black coffee until it is light enough to see
A crossword puzzle. Blue jays,
As many as five raucous in a big holly.
The runners pop in the dark and stream by.
Women in pairs, some pushing strollers.
Power walking, Elkins jump-starts his day.
So these specific lives merge, become
A river, as I watch from the bank—
She's standing alone out on a train platform.
The future. There's a lot of life
Yet to go, and grandkids are not our kids.

TWO KINDS OF PEOPLE

There are those
Who wave until
We are
Out of sight

And others
Who wave, then turn
When we
Start the car

BETH HART, TREMENDOUS BLUES

But Hart not exactly my type.
I start her DVD, *Front and Center,*
2018 NYC. Cruise familiar
Songs until Hart launches into
"Tell Her You Belong to Me."
Not about a lover, but her father,
And a woman he left his family, daughter
For. Next, "I Leave the Light On,"
Scary dark, cigarette burns on arms.
She belts out song after song.
And so, I'm thinking, how little
We know, how little we know.
In her cage, she's singing her ass off—
Tattooed, fierce, her blue eyes.

IT'S BEEN A GOOD DAY

In the Walmart lot, an Hispanic
Family, stranded by their broken Buick
Several states away from home.
So I helped them with a fifty.
I had nothing else good to do with it.

*

When a turtle closed up his house
On the honking road, I quickly stopped—
Looking both ways, extracted him,
Ferried him across. Our lucky
Day, we could have been squashed.

SATURATED GROUND

The phone rang twice Saturday,
Mother Marsh, an old black
Nun I've helped, and Jerene.
Sunday, the phone napped.
This morning, well before 7,
A friend, R. The day previous
She'd seen a Superbowl ad
About children lost too early.
When five years ago I told R.
About Erin, she erupted
In a wail of pure grief.
I told R. my eyes had seeped
All weekend, not weeping,
Just emotions surfacing
Like water in saturated ground.

II.

ERIN

Last Thursday, I sat on your ground
In a cold rain and am still chilled.
Today, you turn twenty-five.
My gorgeous girl, I stand and my face
Comes apart, I want to howl.
I'm freshening your flowers, pink roses,
Your favorite. Beside you
Mother and Daddy and Uncle Mike.
A little girl, you ambushed me
Each night arriving home from work,
Hiding, then vaulting into my lap.
Just last month in Brooklyn, you
And I took off adventuring.
Wandering the Bronx Zoo in a drizzle.
You caught the brooding eyes
Of the Silverback, glued to my side.

GIRL TALKING TO A DOLL

Toys-R-Us

Out shopping for a present
For the first birthday of my first
Grandchild, Swep V—
Blocks, animal puzzles, trucks—
Rounding a corner I surprise
Her, sitting in the aisle.

She looks up, calm, dark eyes.

She's gone, I'm following
Saying Baby, wait, Baby wait.

WHY I LIVE ALONE

I live alone in a big house
With Erin's cat, Mr. P.
When she died two years ago,
He was an ornery fourteen.
I drive out to the cemetery
A few times a month now,
Sit on the ground by Erin's stone.
I tell Erin I love her.
She knows, but likes hearing
Me say it. I tell her I love her
Every day, all day long.
She rolls her eyes, is gone.

AT JUST DUSK, SIPPING BOURBON IN THE YARD

A striped cat, real against the horizon,
 A lean, silk-furred rodent,
With a cock of head turns to spy me,
 Two ivory fangs bared,
Then startles off toward the woods.
 A gouge at the neck's base,
I shake and break the spell of myself,
 Riven clean to the meat.
Push stiffly in chase from my chair.
 Fur, skin, tissue, laid back
Mouth stuffed, he rolls when run down,
 To a quiet, deep-red meat.
I grasp him by his neck's skin-handle,
 One dry gash, enough
In wringing sling a twist of hide free.
 To stop a rat's small heart.

SUSAN

You make me want to be in this world.

FOR S., 8 POEMS

1.   Still Wanting

Both with grown children,
We're surprised by this chance
At love. You're stunning,
High cheekbones, hazel eyes.
Naughty, a girl I want,
Calls every few hours, meeting
Atlanta, Jackson, Oxford.
You starting to call me *Baby*.

                    —*Summer 2012*

2.   New Mexico

We chose Taos to winter.
First morning, sick, S went back
To bed. I wandered, cafes,
Bookstores, and a mineral shop
Where I spent an hour hunting
A gift to please her.
Examined thunder eggs, geodes,
Then a trilobite, back plates
Overlapping like samurai armor.
Her eyes a cool fire, half
Smile, "Since I was a girl, I've
Always wanted a trilobite."

3.   Butter

Breakfast was real oatmeal
Every morning in Taos,
Served at the kitchen table
By the window. Ravens
In the courtyard.
You always put a dab of butter
In my bowl, covered it
So it would melt completely.

4.   Understanding

You slipped into the study,
I followed, locking the door.
Your sarong at your feet,
Hazel eyes, serene, oval face,
Golden hair all in a swirl.
Now—eased—on your side,
Still coming in ripples, you
In the cove of my arms.
I whisper, *Just the beginning.*
"Baby, too fast," you say.
I grab a fistful of damp hair.
Your nails rake my cheek.

—New Year's Eve, Taos

5.   Before Redressing

You asked me to use
Capsaicin on a crusty place
On the nape of your neck.
Naked on bed's edge
You pushed up, held your hair
As I applied the cream.
Carefully, I flaked bits off
Without tearing flesh,
Cleaning, until new skin.
I blew flakes away.
You shivered—then turned,
Of a sudden, *so so* shy.

6.   Your Massage

Easing you back, I remove
Your flats, black hose.
Now, pressing thumbs hard,
Work heel to toes between
The fine bones of each foot.
I kiss, our eyes meeting,
The inside of your right calf,
Your left knee, yet rising.

7.   When We're Gone

I wish you hadn't deleted
The 600+ messages we shared,
Cavafy, koans, fiesty sex.
I smiled, laughed out loud
At your puns, double entendres
Every time I reread them.
Your daughters, my sons,
Not horrified, might have found
Intriguing the kind of people
We were that year—the future
Eerily beautiful—a glyph-
Lined canyon, then horizon.

8.   After

Red bison, black stags, frozen
In firelight on a cave wall.
And, beneath the gallery, there,
Not together, a blond woman,
A dark-eyed man. This cave
A place of memories, we've come
To revisit the past. A past
Not resolved, only abandoned.

LUXURIES

S. liked the "sex,"
the sweetness of "Baby,"
having "a partner,"
but in the end, these
were just luxuries,
ones that she had proved
over a lifetime
she could live without.

WOMAN I WANT, DREAMS

I want to feel safe, she whispers.
I want to curl up in your heart.
Her eyes challenge and engage mine.
"Even if we were consigned to hell, hand
In hand, I'd return us to the light,
Myriad demons scattered, kicking."
She scoffs, a romantic bastard, huh.
"A three-level treehouse high
In an island oak and orangutans."
Hmm, persistent. I like that.
A secret leafy, airy space all our own,
You with friends to tell stories to.

    for S.

TO YOU, NOW

As my eyes open
Behind my closed lids,
Scanning the innerscape.
Moving by thought,
But not too quickly.
My eyes on the horizon,
Forward the only way to go.
I feel you feeling me,
Wondering what
Do we do from here?
I'm thinking, hand
In hand, we start anew.

for S.

III.

OWL

1. My beautiful two-toned friend,
    Your horned head no longer grinds,
    Your eyes shivering light.
    There's rust on your short-hooked beak,
    Your breast feathers run with slime.
    I can't even tell how you fell.

2. Turning the bird with my toe,
    No sudden flush,
    No zephyr-like rush to vacant air,
    No blur-to-dot and gone.

3. Each car rocking the gray road
    Blasts a hot wind,
    Spreading the owl's wing,
    Which falls like a broken accordion.

GULF

Shoulder to shoulder,
In a rough surf, they ride
A yellow raft,
My mother and father.

At the first drops
Of the storm, their faces
Side by side,
They're slow to move.

Legs trailing, now
Propelled, now withdrawn,
They reappear
Each time farther out.

The rhythm of the sea—
I complain it's pulling me
Down—the rhythm
Is my parents' own.

Hugging the raft,
They wear the distant smile
Of those quietly
Listening at a shell.

LITTLE SISTER

for Lisa

1.

Back home, reading in the yard.
Looking up, your hand quietly extending,
"Here," and a creamy fuscata
Bud rolls into my cupped palm.

I balance, eye the bud, inhale.
You slip silently away,
Climb singly the red porch steps,
Vanish within the dark house.

2.

Your hand withdrew, you stepped back.
Very still, just beyond reach,
You poised, a girl at seventeen,
Lovely, on the edge of doubt.

Air filled where you'd stood.
An evasive scent swirled.
And I, sitting on, turning the bud,
Its slow skin, felt   *yours.*

SOMEWHERE IN TENNESSEE

A gum tree suspends
Hundreds of spiny balls
By stems.

The balls rock
In a snowy wind,
Counting time.

There are a limited number
Of such trees on the planet.
I cannot disclose
To you my location
So delicate
Is the balance.

A CEILING BAS-RELIEF

The Fontaine House

1. 1850. To typhus, the only boy
of a tinsmith, lost. Off to the side
of the mourning, swinging its
neck, the child's pet swan rejects
food, follows its small master.
The smith resumes work. Borne
by river Natchez to Memphis,
across years he labors, ornamenting
the homes of the wealthy.
In 1870, to this house, comes.

2. Atop a scaffold, face uplifted,
Kneeling. He applies
A thin base. An oval frame
Molds. Hands floating,
The curved outline of wings
Forms, feather by feather
Details. Now,
                    between the wings,
Eyes, a delicate nose—

Stare: the smith's hands
        long since air,

Lively, this face with his jaw.

JERENE

1.   You selected the worm-blind runt
        From a poisoned bitch's litter,
        Cried when colic straightened it,
        Nursed odd hours into the night,
        Suspended the bare-gummed pup
        Between your will and death.

2.   This morning at the 3 a.m. check,
        You found it warm with life,
        But a strange bloom in its gut,
        Stretched limp with mouth agape.

3.   You wrapped it in a torn sheet,
        In the ease of your arms held it,
        Watched as I spaded the earth.
        Stayed, even as it began to rain.

PAWPAW: JULY 1935

No movement but for the waves of heat
Shivering up from the street in blurry S's.
He draws the stiff shades,
Awkwardly, bolts the office door.

Now, clients barred, back to the reading
Room, where from tomes of law
Lining three walls, he turns to a small
Shelf, scans the volumes
Of The Great Works of Literature:
Pope underlined; Thoreau derided
In a margin; Darwin considered, as face
Flat, the binding settled so to attest.

He uncaps, tips a flask of bourbon.
Today, it's *Don Quixote* that he's chosen.
By the clock, just noon.
In amber, an air-pocket, this room.

OF JEREMY, AGE 2

My 5 a.m. shower done,
Exiting the bathroom door,

And an intruder stares,
His blond head centering my
Pillow, squinting
At the sudden light.

Not to wake my wife,
On her side, breathing evenly,
I growl softly,
"Who comes to my bed?"

He smiles, then gray
Eyes closing, turns his face
Away,
Through darkness

Drifting loved toward day.

THIS MORNING, 5/5/03

This morning, I'm calling my
Little sister to get my little brother's
Phone number.
Then I remember, Mike's dead.

This morning, I'm listening
To Lucinda Williams and wondering
How I've managed
To help so little those around me.

This morning, the boys and I,
Cocoa, a chocolate lab, Coal, a wolfhound,
And Lola, a St. Bernard,
We're up and down the upstairs
Porch, barking at everything.

Sometimes the world
Is too beautiful, and I'm full to bursting—
This morning, 5/5/03.

PASSAGE

Entering the woods, the path rose to our feet,
The earth firm and cool, beneath latticed
Branches. We walked years in this way,
Occasionally hand in hand, more often
Without touching, though sensing presence.
Then, subtly, the path's composition
Began changing. Now, rounding an oak,
Thick brush prevents our rejoining.
I start to call to her, but there's a birdsong
I haven't heard in years, a flash
Of exotic color high in the feathery
Branches. Wandering, beside a stream I stop.
In the bright water cupped in my hands
My face. And I, who since a youth
Sought an overview so as to synthesize,
I search the dark-eyed reflection only
To recognize, not admire myself. My instinct
Is a shout to her, but if we follow voices
To blend our dotted paths on farther
In the wood, what can change?
Crisply, a car door slams. I look out.
She has returned in her green car, and I rise,
Unclasping my intertwined fingers,
The crystal I've stared into, becoming air.

WE SPLIT THE DALIS

She got Chagall's *Cirque Soleil*.
I got the four Friedlaenders.
We split the Dalis, *Helen of Troy*
And *Kissing Grapes*, with its glittered
Angel, bough of purple skulls.
So we move, bedroom
To bedroom, dining to living room,
Pulling art off walls. But not until
The den, when I reach to lift
Alvar's *Espacio Rojo*—our first auction—
Does she break down, face
In hands, sink to the blue couch.
I closed my eyes. Returned,
Backtracking, each piece to its home.
All the days, the nights, room
After room of memories on fire.

9 MONTHS DIVORCED

Jan. 2006, another year of hope,
And I run into Jerene exiting
Gould's Spa. I offer to buy
Her a coffee, and she accepts.
We two alone in the corner cafe,
We sit on and on, sipping,
Me staring as if to memorize
Her face. I ask if I make her
Uncomfortable. She says no,
Just wonders what I'm thinking.
She says, I'm getting older,
I know it. To which I say, yes.
My mind runs back through
The years. The face, the high
Cheekbones, the green eyes
That seized and held mine fast
As I gawked that first day
In the catacombs in Vienna.
So, so beautiful, even as
You have been each and every
One of these past thirty years.

SELF-PORTRAIT

Jan. 2, of this year of hope,
2005. Sixty degrees in Memphis,
On the retreat that is my upstairs
Porch, me, and Lola barking
At first one runner, then another.
I'm drinking bourbon, 9:30
In the morning, I've recorded
That fact before, listening
To the CD Jeremy burned for me,
"Big John," "The Devil Went Down
To Georgia," stirring songs.
Inside, a telephone jangles.
Looking out over woods soaked
By a night of rain, and it
Still drizzling, I give a long wolf
Howl—now, turn to answer.

MAZE

From the bright world into the black
Entrance he disappeared,
But darkness was an old companion,
And besides, he prided himself
On his composure. Pupils growing,
He drove ever inward until, deep
Within the echoing maze, he realized
He was lost. His jaw set,
He shouted for the Minotaur, its
Heated breath, foam-flecked nostrils.
He'd command the beast to lead
Him back to the light.
      Outside,
At each bellow, the crowd shivered
To imagine what dwelt within.

BEEN DOWN SO LONG
IT LOOKS LIKE UP TO ME

A short novel by Richard Fariña.
Fariña declared himself "exempt"
From possession by demons, and also
Generally, in life. Intrigued,
S. too assumed the status, decided
To test the premise, "exempt"
Brought the demons to life
In his own head. Couldn't sleep.
Couldn't turn out the lights at night
Without panic, which he rode
The waves of. Then, six days,
Black nights, mumbling, and pacing,
In Louisiana camping alone.
To the side, the demons yet reside.
Rising to mix another drink,
S. really doesn't want them loosed,
Though today, bored, he wonders
If he's still as strong as Hell.

GRACE

Mother, eighty-four, took Uncle
James for a ride yesterday.
Drove her brother to the cemetery
To visit Daddy and Mike.
After, she called their flowers lovely,
Then asked, "Where's Daddy?
Where is my husband?"

*

For the first time in fifteen years
I dream of Mike, him driving up
In Mother's big Oldsmobile,
Then waiting. We talk, he nods.
Now, I realize he has come
For Mother. As the old ones say,
To take her home. I go to her
Bed, grab her hand. I'm waking,
Mother's hand cooling in mine.

April 15, 2009

Today, my little sister and I
Will go to select a coffin
For Mother. Eighteen years ago,
I went with Mother to choose
Mike's. Yesterday, my mother died.
Like a kaleidoscope twisted
And twisted, the world
Broken, scattered bits of glass.

*

I dreamed of Mother a couple
Of nights ago. She was blond
And slim, walking by a lake.
The dream was in slow motion,
Washed in silver. A ballet.
A friend offers, she wants you
To know everything's okay,
That in death we're young again.
And me, the dead don't look
Back, that is their earned grace.

IV.

REPORT TO THE BOYS

Yes, I crossed over.
Saw Maha and Granddaddy
Drinking coffee under trees.
I have loved you, Swep—
You, Jeremy—each and every day
Since you were born.
Always, Jerene, and Erin—
Who one midnight called
From NY, asked, "Dad, when
Are you going to give up
On me?" "Never, Baby."
I sired sons, Swep and Jeremy,
And a daughter, Erin.
Who at fifteen sold me her
Poems, $5 apiece.

TRILOBITE

Lisa called from a mineral shop
In Nashville—a trilobite.
I gave a long-held, treasured one
To R., later replaced it in Taos,
Which became a gift for S.
So a trilobite awaits a quester
To take it up, weigh it in her hand.
An ancient token, a passage
Into a world evolving as I type.

FIFTEEN YEARS LATER

Jerene's moved to a house,
A nice area, that Jeremy bought for her.
"I must've done something right."
She sold our house. Has gotten a dog.
We always had 2-5 as the boys
And Erin grew up. Lola, the last
And our favorite, a St. Bernard, died
Five years ago. So Jerene's gotten
A dog, a four-month old
St. Bernard—Violet. Puppies are
Rebirths of a sort. Jerene and Violet
Walk mornings, puppy-park
Afternoons. I told Jerene, moments
Ago, you have another baby
To raise. "That's right," she said.
Life is both hopeless and beautiful.
My heart is heavy, light. Both.

MESSAGES

Z. wrote a poem about a man
Who sat not to write poems
But to message with the world.
She, of course, nailed it.
I did an interview for the local
Paper, *The Daily Leader.*
The reporter asked why I wrote.
I said to find people like me.
My poems are messages,
Put into bottles, thrown out beyond
The breakers, as far as I can.
So I have watched, waited,
For her who has fished a bottle
From the sea, at my door,
Come to return a poem to me.

REBECCA

Her hair tied up, Bible in bag,
From Wednesday night
Meeting—walking fast, ever faster—
She ducks into a honky-tonk,
Jerry's Place, by the side door.
Weaving to a scarred
Steinway, she seats herself. Tests
The keyboard, end-to-end
Tinkling. Now, head tilting
Back, with a quick breath, she starts
To bang, to raise Cain, hair
Whipping in the bar's dark air.

THOSE DAYS, FRIDAYS

Rushing in from Memphis
I'd fumble with my key
And surprise! just inside
The door, blood lips, smoky
Raccoon eyes, You.
From the rear, your favorite,
Snugly we fit together.
Your little giggle, *Baby
Bingo, Bingo, Bingo Baby.*
Then, I came, pumping
My need deep into you.
Asserting my claim, again.

For R

JULY 4, 2008

Fireworks starring black sky,
Red, blues, yellows.
Drinking wine in the church
Parking lot. Standing
Behind you, hands in your hair,
Sliding my hands from neck
To collarbone, running over
The swell of your breasts
To pinch your nipples, stars.

for R.

CURTAINS DRAWN

Shucking her tee shirt,
She takes *him* first
In fist, then in teasing mouth.
She enjoys her power.
He tenses, his back arches.
Smiling, she has promised
To drain him dry,
Now rhythmically does.
She slides up. Her head
On his chest. On and on
They lie, alone in the world
And outside time, Eden.

    for R.

BANSHEE

Kate Bush

Reading my poems in London.
A woman in a dark cowl,
The front row. I'm sharing
Words that are colors, feelings,
Like mescaline. The event
Is ending, K. says
I've initialed 50 books
In your stead,
Apologize that they aren't
Personalized, and give them
Those. She's humming
"Wuthering Heights,"
Taking my hand, saying, Let's
Get something to eat.
She's thinking, after a little
Sustenance,
I want you to love me.

BROOKHAVEN

Jerene brought Swep V and Cannon
To Brookhaven for a few days.
The boys explored the yard, and back lot,
Pilfered the playhouse, the attic,
Dragging out old junk, broken toys, etc.
And then, the highlight, Saturday
Night and the Exchange Club Fair
Their daddy had loved going to as a boy.
Cannon tossed and tried to ring
Little bowls with goldfish.
Swep dunked the clown at the dunk tank,
Centering the target with a fast ball.
The tilt-a-whirl three times,
Twice, the roller coaster, the Ferris wheel.
The nightcap, the train that creaked
As it circled the whole park.
Before they left, I offered Jerene
Some auction jewelry to sort through.
She, emerald earrings, chose.
Thought, 40 years, the marriage done,
And still, this fierce afterglow.